A Soldier At Last

By

Linda Sullivan

Edited by David Miller

Published by

Abernant Publishing
58 Coopers Rise
Godalming
Surrey GU7 2NJ

ISBN 978-1-909196-12-4

Printed and bound
in the United Kingdom by

Think Ink Fine Art Printers

11-13 Philip Road
Ipswich
Suffolk IP2 8BH

I dedicate this book to my two daughters,
Karen & Kelly for all your help, especially
in the latter years of my life.

Linda Sullivan

CONTENTS

POST WAR

I was born in July of 1946 in what was called the Baby Boom era, a post war baby, except my Father did not go to war. He was classed as medically unfit and continued to work as a builder in the trade he knew and was highly skilled at it. He was a Welshman nicknamed "Taff", his name was a good welsh name Griffith Augustus Berry. He spent his childhood in a mining town in the Rhonda Valley, not being looked after well as his Mother died, and his father couldn't always feed the children properly, this led to my Father's ill health; and although a handsome man with black wavy hair and a gentle but firm nature with my older sister Janet, and my Mother, he lost his life tragically on a Christmas Eve as a result of a heart attack, he was 35. He died having collapsed on a bus stop coming home from work.

This was my first ever Christmas, I was five months old and Janet aged five. What a Christmas that must have been for my Mother, Olive; she opened the door to a Policeman who came to tell her the sad news. When I was born my Mother had longed for a boy, and when she was told "Another daughter, what will you call her", she was so disappointed she replied

"Linda – just plain Linda!" So I have no middle name. But she loved me all the same and did her very best in the circumstances.

DAD

You died when I was five months old
On a Christmas Eve
That Christmas it was bleak and cold
I was too young to grieve

So Dad I've never known the touch
Of your arms around me
A Father's guidance I missed so much
Years on, I'm over sixty

But all through life I hope I've been
The girl you loved with pride
During my marriage, motherhood, and joys
I longed for you by my side.

I only know stories from others before
Who say you were the best

What I'd give to see you, love you more
And wish "Happy Father's day" like the rest.

We lived with my Grandparents, Alice & Jos (Josiah), who had bought the house when they married. My parents were planning to have a bungalow built, but of course that never happened., and Mum was left a young widow. She worked hard looking after my elderly grandparents, plus working as a box maker in a local chocolate factory. We became a close family and I loved Alice & Jos, Gran and Granfer I called them. Gran was so kind to me, I would sit on her ample lap on which she wore her cross-over pinny, and she would rub my hands and show me such love and warmth; and tell me stories.

Granfer was a gentle man dominated by Gran, who ruled the roost really. He wore a cloth cap in the house, and a muffler around his neck, and sat in a large wooden high backed chair, smoking his pipe and talking about his life working in the pottery. He played rugby and cricket in his younger days and enjoyed a pint at the local, and a game of cribbage in the cribbage team at the pub. He taught me to play crib at an early age, and my ambition in those days was to become part of the "team". I liked all card games, and when Gran & Granfer were tired of playing I would play patience on their table.

They were in the front room of the house, where a big double bed dominated the room. There were two armchairs, and a table in front of the window, and a huge ornate sideboard. Both suffered with arthritis therefore they couldn't climb the stairs. I loved to go to see them early in the morning and snuggle up between them in their big bed.

At the age of three my Mother married my stepfather, Wilf, a man much older than herself, who had lived in the little street behind our house, just in front of the railway line. He was a widower and always very kind to me. The marriage was not a happy one, as I remember them arguing a great deal. He was also unfortunately ill, so their marriage only lasted seven years when he died when I was ten.

By now Gran & Granfer had deteriorated in health, suffering a few strokes each, and dementia in Granfer. Mum was so very tired looking after everyone single-handed. She was a good cook and we all relished the lovely home cooking she produced; a skill my sister and I have valued. We can both produce an elaborate meal when required, and enjoy cooking very much. Mum was a great pastry cook, and her apple pies & Jam tarts were enjoyed by all the family. If we misbehaved a look from her was enough, and we knew we had overstepped the mark.

Janet and Linda

EARLY YEARS

My early years were enhanced by my membership of the Salvation Army. Mum and her two brothers had attended as children, and later my uncles played in the band. Gran was a tailoress and had made many uniforms for the old Fishponds Corps. I went to Sunday School with Janet, and I loved the music of the "Army" from an early age, wanting to be more involved as I grew up. Firstly I joined the Singing Company and became a junior soldier. Then I joined the Timbrel band, I wore a uniform with coloured tassels fixed diagonally across the front, the same colours as the ribbons on our tambourines. I still have my tambourine with the ribbons connected, and love to accompany a good old "march" when I am on my own at home. The music of the Salvation Army lifts my spirit, and gladdens my soul. I remember my years in the Army as enjoyable and special times, becoming part of a wider family that filled a void in my life.

Each summer we went on a coach trip for our Sunday School outing to Weston-Super-Mare. It was always the same, and every year the coach would break down, in the end we expected it to happen and it always did!

At Christmas time in the Sunday School hall, long trestle tables were erected and decorated, and the most marvellous tea was provided for us all. By the time I was fifteen I was being slightly pressurised to wear senior soldier uniform, and sign the senior soldier's pledge. I was a Sunday school teacher by this time. I had my doubts, and mentioned my reservations. I will continue this story at a later stage.

Harvest Festival was a much loved occasion, with wonderful music from the band and songs from the Songsters. All married or related to someone else in the Corp, one big family. One boy Ken, who lived in our street, came to Sunday School. We joined a procession to the mercy seat in the main hall. Normally quite a plain hall but now decorated with sheaves of corn, a harvest loaf, and vegetables grown in our families allotments. Granfer always supplied us with a huge marrow. We would have a basket or box filled with our harvest fare to offer. Ken had a rather long wait one year and by the time he'd reached the front, all that was left was pips and cores of the fruit he had brought. The following year his Mother gave him a box of tinned goods! "Lead us not into temptation" would have suited Ken well!

My faith which was nurtured and grew in my early years is with me today, and has sustained me through my life. Not having a "normal" family life with a mother & Father, I'm sure I gained great strength from the characters I came to trust and know in the Army.

We would have Officers for perhaps three or four years and then they would move on, I sometimes made great friends with their children and felt very sad when they moved away.

THE ARMY

The "Army" has a special place
In my heart throughout the years
When I go to a meeting and sit in my place
I brush away the tears!

I think of how as a child of two
I was in the old Fishponds Corp
I proudly showed them my new shoes!
Many people then were so poor.

I always had a lot to say
Of words I was never afraid
But I learnt to sing, and also to pray
And joined the timbrel brigade

Diagonal coloured cords we adorned so nimble
On our blouses from left to right
They matched the ribbons on our timbrel
We lifted as high as a kite!

Every meeting I'm left with a warm glow
That's what the "Army" does for you
The welcome and greeting the Officers show
Cheers you up if you feel blue

I've lapsed a lot throughout the years
And worshipped in many places
But I love to visit the Army at times
The joy is so evident on faces.

The band, and juniors play so sweet
The tunes are always so happy
To listen along and beat with your feet
And sometimes feel moved to be clappy!

I never did get the bonnet to wear
It was always my ambition
Now bonnets are out, they were so fair!
Now they are only a remonition.

Even the plainest lady looked good
In the bonnet with the bow
Although old-fashioned to keep they should
Their good features it would show

You have to keep abreast with the times
Be modern and in tune
I've tried to keep this all in rhyme!
I'll finish very soon!

Just to end I'd like to state
The "Army's" in my soul
The music always is first rate
Blood and Fire reigns the pole.

SCHOOLDAYS

I cannot remember a great deal about infant school, except it was there I met my best friend Jane, who is still my friend today, and Godmother to my daughter, Kelly. We moved on to a mixed secondary modern school where I enjoyed my school life.

My favourite lessons were English and cookery. I was made a prefect as I showed organising ability. A teacher took me under his wing and encouraged me to start a school magazine, which meant lots of ground work. I was studying for my U.E.I. Examination, the forerunner of G.C.E., but managed to fit everything in. This involved interviewing, typing reports, and printing the magazine when completed. We designed the cover and stapled the lot together, and sold them to raise funds for the school. I wanted to be a journalist, and this teacher suggested to my Mum I should go to College. She declined, saying she could not afford to extra expense, there were no grants in those days. I left school at sixteen, and went to work in an office. Whilst at school I helped to organise school dances, and never being short of a boyfriend used to enjoy "bopping" to the records in the school hall. We thought we were so cool!

Jane & I one day went to the Library to do our homework. It was the early 60's and we dressed up in our mini skirts and stockings which were supported by suspenders. In the Library the chairs were typically 60's style, white plastic covered metal rod frames, open design. In those days Libraries were silent places, where a cough was frowned upon! We spent a long while writing our essays and I attempted to rise from the chair, taking it with me hitched to my suspender! We couldn't talk for giggling, and doubled up as I tried to release the chair and couldn't. We still remember the incident and laugh about it together.

Around this time I required pocket money for the usual items teenage girls want to buy. Fashionable clothes, make up, records and magazines, so I looked around for a Saturday job. Just around the corner from our house was a ladies hairdressing salon.

I worked there for around three years, working more hours in my school holidays. I would neutralise the perms, make appointments, take payments, sweep up, and generally make myself useful, keeping everyone supplied with tea and coffee. There were no blow dries in those days, just wash and sets, drying under the domed dryers with hairnets on! It was all very adult conversation about husbands, holidays and children, and I was happy to be part of it. I wore a white nylon coat and it smelt of ammonia & perm lotion. I learnt a lot about hair care and gave myself home perms thereafter with no problem. The money was so useful as Mum couldn't afford to give me the little extra's. Pat, the owner, was always going to Portugal on holiday, and I loved to hear about the faraway places, and dream I would visit them one day.

I loved writing, and constantly wrote articles to the local paper. The children's page was called the Sunshine Club, and Uncle Will ran the Club. I frequently saw my name in print, and sometimes drawings or poems I had sent in. I loved to enter competitions, and sometimes would win a book. I also gained a penfriend in Australia called Inez arranged through the Sunshine Club, and wrote to her for many years.

The holiday we had annually was usually a week at Weston-Super-Mare. My great uncle owned a car, and would take us there and collect us a week later. Mum would buy the food and we stayed with a lady whom we called Auntie Ethel. She owned the tiny house, and she would cook the food Mum bought. I remember it was near the floral clock, we watched the mechanical bird emerge on the hour and tweet. One year during my Mother's second marriage we went to Brighton, with my Mother, Stepfather, his brother and wife. Janet & I sat outside of pubs extremely bored with a bag of crisps and lemonade. The holiday certainly didn't revolve around the children as our holidays did after my marriage.

AMAMI NIGHT

Friday nights were amami nights, they were such fun! Mum, Janet & I would keep this special evening for our weekly pamper session. Nothing like the pamper nights of this age, ours were primitive and simple, and hard work for my Mother. She would drag the tin bath in front the coal fire in our back room. We would take it in turns to have a bath, adding more hot water and bath salts each time one of us stepped inside. Our hair would be washed in the kitchen sink using a jug, and Mum would wind her hair around dinkie curlers and place a net over to hold the curls intact until the next morning.

Amami would be combed through before curling or putting in rollers. Mum always asked one of us to pluck her eyebrows, and sometimes we would apply a facemask to purify our skin. All three of us had the advantage of thick brown hair, and a greasy complexion, which in later life would be a bonus of not showing too many lines! If we were expecting to go somewhere special at the weekend we would manicure our nails, and apply nail varnish. Never in a bright colour, mostly clear varnish.

Mum (Olive), Janet & Linda

CHRISTMAS TIME

Apart from the sadness each Christmas Eve, we always managed to enjoy our simple Christmas's. Mum would buy a small real tree and it would be placed in a corner alcove in the back room. We would fix candle holders to the branches, and these would hold real candles which Mum would light with a match. The thought now puts shivers down my spine, health & safety unknown! We would use the same plastic ornaments and fairy lights year after year. Handmade paper decorations were pinned to the wall using drawing pins. As a special treat Mum bought me each year a bottle of cordial, it looked like a bottle of wine, and I would be served it in a tiny glass, feeling very grown-up. I've never found out what it was called, or made from, but I loved the taste. Not much money could be spent on presents but we appreciated the little we had. Sometimes the Salvation Army would come to an open-air meeting and stand outside Gran's window playing carols. Although my Mother had attended the Army as a child she didn't wear uniform, so the adults in the family enjoyed a drink. Snowball was a favourite one, made from Advocaat and lemonade, with a cherry.

Janet chose to attend an all girls school, but I liked the boys too much to choose the same. At school I met a boy called John, we started going out with each other when I was thirteen. I was a serious and mature minded teenager so it didn't seem that I was too young. We dated for three years, all but a short break for a few months, when I saw quite a few other boys. John was an only child of elderly parents, they owned a holiday caravan at Blue Anchor bay near Minehead, and we all used to go on holiday there. John seemed sensible and mature until I started work, and then compared to other men I met, he suddenly appeared immature and childish.

Janet had just married and I was to be bridesmaid. Gran & Granfer had died recently and life at home was changing rapidly. I missed my grandparents so much. Mum was working in a greengrocers shop, and had a new man in her life. There was an emptiness now. At work one of the mechanics called Mike was giving me lots of compliments and asking me to go out with him. So unfortunately, I gave John the old "heave-ho" and ended our friendship. Mike was someone older and I knew he would look after me. I was sixteen but felt like twenty. I loved sewing, knitting and cooking and soon I realised I wanted to settle down with Mike in a home of our own. Where we would both work hard to perhaps give our children what we hadn't had.

I had always been reminded at school that I was from a one parent family. Free dinners and special concessions. My Mum would tell people "she hasn't got a daddy", and I suppose I felt incomplete somehow. Now I found a chance of happiness and a life I could control, where I would be cared for and I would put as much energy into married life as I could.

MIKE

Mike told me his father was in hospital dying when I met him. I did visit him once in hospital, but it was only weeks after our first courtship that he passes away. Ironically, it was on a Christmas Eve, as my Dad had died., and although my Mother had never met Mike's Father, I dreaded going home that day to give her the news. She had always relived that terrible day every Christmas Eve.

Mike's Mother, Kathleen, had died giving birth to Mike, so he never knew her, as I had not known my Father. His Grandmother sold her home and brought him up, together with his older brother by ten years. She looked after them, and Mike's Father, which wasn't easy, as after Kathleen's death he drank heavily. He was epileptic so he should not have mixed the drink with his medication. Mike remembers him constantly having blackouts and falling about, sometimes in the fire. He couldn't work so money was scarce. Mike's brother married, and Mike was the only breadwinner. He had a great deal of responsibility at an early age, and wanted to look after Gran as she had looked after him. He called her "Mum", as she was the only Mum he knew.

Together, we were determined to make our children's lives so different from our own and I hope we have achieved that. The children these days cannot imagine the hardships we endured because they have had it so easy. Our children had a holiday every year with us until they left home, but Mike didn't know what it was to go on holiday.

He tells the story of when he was at school. The teacher told the class to write an essay on what they had done in the summer holiday. Because he had gone nowhere, Mike made up an unbelievable story and wrote it. The teacher called him out in front of the class and smacked his face for telling untruths. His Gran had always told him to "turn the other cheek" so he did – to the teacher, who was taken aback by his attitude. He asked Mike questions why, and when mike explained he had never been on a holiday, the teacher arranged a week on a farm for Mike to enjoy. This has always stayed in his memory.

Gran was a genteel lady, very well spoken and caring. She loved Mike a great deal and he loved her. She was 62 when he was born and lived until she was 93. He painted the house they lived in, outside and inside before we married, and made sure she was comfortable. Her husband died when Mike was a baby, and two of her children lived nearby. Her son, Arthur was blind, and was married to a blind lady, it was marvellous how they managed. We visited them frequently. The daughter, Cissie lived nearby with her husband. She also suffered with her sight, and after her husband died she lived in a home for the blind.

Mike

THE MID SIXTIES

Mike had the use of the firm's van, so we would often go to look at how the first Severn Bridge was progressing, at Aust. Once we drove through the Severn bore which had flooded the van. Our feet got soaking wet as the water gushed in the van. He was very conservative in his clothes, and wore arm braces to keep his shirt sleeves up as he was small in stature. I loved him from the start and it wasn't long before we became serious about one another and thinking of marriage. I left working for the office machine company, and I worked for a time as a receptionist in an Opticians, and then an Orthodontist in the City.

We courted for three years, after a year we became engaged, and then saved to buy a house, he was concerned about leaving his Gran but we knew in the end we wanted to be on our own.

Just after I started going out with Mike my Mother went into hospital for a thyroid operation. We were in a pub having a drink when the Officer from the Salvation Army came in selling the War Cry. I guiltily sped to the Ladies, but he spotted me! And when we arrived home a War Cry was left in the door. Mike enjoyed a drink, and when I met him I was deliberating whether to be a Senior Soldier, and sign the pledge. Mum said it wouldn't work if we both were not committed and I thought she was right. So I eventually left the Army, and teased Mike he had caused me to be thrown out for drinking!

When our banns were read in his Church, which was the Church of England I couldn't understand the service, and commented to his Gran that I didn't see any point in all the standing up and sitting down every few minutes. It was quite a high church. I would later realise the significance of the responses in the Church of England service.

I missed my Sundays at the Army but I had so much now to fill my weekends with. We made the most of weekends as during the week we only saw each other on Tuesday and Thursday evenings. We were saving hard so there wasn't a lot of entertainment we wished to pursue.

Janet & Pete, her husband lived in a residential caravan, and each Thursday evening we would visit them, we would all watch Peyton Place on their television. Just as we were planning our wedding they were expecting their first baby, Janet had miscarried the first baby. She was my Matron of Honour, but her pregnancy didn't show in her bridesmaids dress.

Me and Mike on our wedding day

CASA MIA

During our engagement we began looking in earnest for a house. Mike serviced camera's in betting shops, and one day he met an Estate Agent who had a house for sale. Mike told me it was being sold complete with furniture, I said I wouldn't want everything second hand so we drove over to say "No".

When we saw the house, it was only four years old, very attractive and modern looking. The owner was divorced and wanted to sell it complete, with fridge, cooker, furniture etc. We changed our mind immediately, as it was in good condition, and a nice home.

The name of the house was "CASA MIA" which means our home. There was a good sized garden and a garage. This was October 1964, and the wedding was to be June 1965. We settled the deal and paid rates on the property as the furniture was in the house.

Today, I am sure, in the same situation a couple would move in together. But it wasn't heard of in those days, so we stayed at home until we married.

Sometimes we would go to the house to check everything was in order, and dream of living there permanently. Mike was interested in carpentry, he made a strong wooden ottoman to take the bed linen, and a radiogram. We were very proud of our new home.

It was not too far from where Mum lived. Mike lived a little further away, he painted and decorated his Gran's house, and also repaired the roof. She took in a lodger for a time, so she wasn't all alone.

THE WEDDING

We married on June 12th 1965, the day was mixed with sunshine and showers. My dress was white broderie anglais, and Janet was in blue. Her husband Pete gave me away. The day was happy, and we travelled to Newquay for our honeymoon.

It was a wet summer, and rained most of the week we were there, but we didn't worry and couldn't wait to begin our married life in our little house. I can remember receiving the proof wedding photographs at the Hotel, and we were handed them at breakfast time. Mike said not to open them until later as everyone would know we were on honeymoon!

Janet left work to have the baby, a little girl Paula on January 6th 1966. Little did I know I would give birth to a daughter on Boxing Day the same year.

During that eighteen months we were busy making the house our home. Mike made a lovely drop sided cot, and we decorated the nursery. Glad of my interest in sewing and knitting I made plenty of clothes in readiness. I felt very sick for quite a few months at the start of my pregnancy. By this time I was working in an office of a large chemist near Temple Meads Station in Bristol. I reduced my hours to part-time, although we needed the money we lived within our means. We could always manage our finances well, and both being practical people we saved a lot making things ourselves. I also loved cooking and we gradually asked everyone who had come to the Wedding to visit us for tea. Sunday teas were famous in our family. My Mother had taught me to make traditional pies, cakes and suchlike. Each Saturday for years would find me in the kitchen making batches of cakes to last the week or feed the visitors.

We also made sure we visited my Mum and Mike's Gran frequently. Uncle Arthur and his wife were blind, and when they visited us for the first time it was interesting to see how they felt the walls to imagine the size. Mike would often attend to jobs which needed to be done at their home. Glaucoma was rife in the family in each generation including the younger members. We were concerned our baby would not be affected, but realised more could be done than in the past.

FAMILY LIFE

Paula, our niece was a treasure and we couldn't wait for our baby to come. I was booked for my GP to deliver the baby at the local cottage hospital. Mike attended the antenatal classes, and wished to be present at the birth. That was what I dearly wanted but it wasn't to be, as I went into labour on the Christmas Eve, was admitted to hospital, and Karen wasn't born until the Boxing Day. All day Christmas Day I was in labour, Mike would stay for a few hours, and then go to tell the family nothing had happened. None of us had telephones at that time.

When Karen finally arrived by forceps to speed the delivery Mike wasn't there. When he did return we were overjoyed with our first baby. I couldn't hold her because of the trauma of the birth, she was placed in her cot for nearly a day. Father Christmas (one of the doctor's) made a ward visit, and gave each of us a parcel of goodies, which included a lovely white and pink fur rabbit. This was to become a particular favourite animal of Karen's, and we later had rabbits as pets, and bred many baby rabbits.

We were lucky enough to have another daughter, Kelly, three years later. Our family was complete, and once again we worked out our finances. Two children were the limit we could afford.

Whilst I was pregnant with Karen we had a holiday in Jersey. It was the first time I had flown, we flew from Bristol and enjoyed our stay on the island. Coming home was a disaster however. The plane couldn't land in Bristol because of the fog, we were forced to sleep on the benches at Jersey airport. It was most uncomfortable especially in my condition. We had spent all our money on duty free to take home prior to the expected return flight. The airport management gave us enough money to buy a meal, and we returned the next day looking the worst for wear, but it didn't put me off flying.

During Karen's first summer we took her to Teignmouth for a holiday. It was good weather and we all enjoyed ourselves. She always needed her sleep and I can remember trying to push her buggy up and down the sands to try to give her a mid-day nap. I made summer dresses for myself and a little one for her to match. This I continued to do for many years, though the girls told me many years hence they hated it! I made their nighties, dressing gowns, dresses and coats to match, and dolly's clothes to match theirs!

Karen was quite an easy baby, she loved her food and wanted to feed herself from an early age. She was late talking, but made herself known to what she wanted some way or another. My Mother was thrilled having two little grand-daughters at just a year difference in age, and then three when Kelly came along. Janet had a boy, Matthew, the year before Kelly was born so every year in stages there was a new baby.

We found our dining-room very small so when Karen was tiny Mike took on the mammoth task of building an extension. The foundations were as deep as the extension itself as the garden is on a slope. It made a tremendous difference, and a little bit more room for the girls to play.

Kelly was born October 1969 at the same hospital. The birth was much easier, and Mike was able to be present. Mum looked after Karen for a couple of weeks, and would bring her into the hospital to see her new sister. At that time Mike's Gran was quite ill, she had fallen and was in hospital so Mike was visiting each of us in turn. She died soon after Kelly's christening, which she attended as a very proud great grand-mother. She was a very special lady and we all remember her with such affection and gratitude for her sacrifices she made for Mike.

RABBITS

When the girls became the age to walk to school on their own they passed a house where the "rabbit man" lived. He was retired and he lived with his wife. In his garage were row upon row of multi-storey hutches he had built. It was a delight for all the children around to stop off and feed the rabbits on the way home from school. Soon Karen & Kelly were asking for a rabbit to have housed in our shed. Mike got to work again building a multi-story hutch, we finally had three. Friskey was the first for Karen, a lovely white ermine rex with long ears and pink eyes just like the rabbit I had been given when Karen was born. Kelly was next to own Bobtail, a netherland dwarf white rabbit. She was smaller for Kelly to handle, and very sweet.

Mr Hancock, the rabbit man was a member of a rabbit club. We became rabbit mad! And soon the girls and their rabbits were winning colourful rosettes at the shows. The rabbits were used to being handled at the show, and judges inspected every nook and cranny, tails, ears and feet to make sure they were good enough to win a rosette. Prior to each show the girls would spend hours brushing the coats and clipping the nails. Mike was adamant this must be their responsibility and I can honestly say that any prizes were to their credit. Each Saturday their friends at school would watch a popular Saturday morning children's programme on television but not Karen & Kelly. They would be shopping for hay and straw and rabbit food, and cleaning the hutches out. We didn't see the point in children owning an animal and shelving the responsibility onto parents.

Breeding was next on the agenda. Mr. Hancock would have Friskey & Bobtail to meet up with a male rabbit of his, and the girls gave lots of care throughout the pregnancy, and what joy when the baby bunnies were born! Mr. Hancock usually knew of a child or a member of the club requiring a rabbit, so we didn't have any problems re-housing them.

At the shows I fell in love with an orange rex, and soon I owned Percy. He didn't live as long as the doe's, I think he wore himself out as he was very frisky and was always ready to mate with a doe. We had all the rabbits for many years, and experienced fun times with them. Mr. Hancock became quite a close friend to Mike.

Soon another interest took up the girl's time at weekends, but they fitted the rabbit cleaning later in the day., and that was ballroom dancing. They attended ballet classes when they were younger and took many exams. Karen enjoyed it more than Kelly, then as they became a little older they asked to go to ballroom dancing. They did most things together, and Karen would take care of Kelly who was a little unsure of herself and not so confident. We bought them dancing shoes, and soon they were entered for medals for dancing. They both did very well and soon we started to take an interest too. One evening a week we would get a babysitter and attend our lessons. We also won medals and eventually the girls and ourselves achieved bronze, silver and gold in modern ballroom and latin American dances. Mike & I loved the Latin, especially the cha-cha and rumba.

About once a month our teachers would hold a Saturday evening family dance. They would organise competitions, and we would have numbers on our backs, and visiting judges would give prizes and trophies to the winners. Many times Mike would win with either Karen or Kelly as his partner. What happy times we had then, as a family with a shared interest and love of dancing and music. The girl's bedrooms were becoming full of medals and trophies for dancing and rabbit shows.

Our teachers announced they were planning a dancing holiday to Torremolinos in Spain for ten days. We had never been abroad so we decided to save hard to take the girls. I worked evenings in a pickle onion factory to earn extra spending money. It was a horrible job, and I would return home reeking of the smell of pickled onions which I had peeled all evening. It was worth it to see the girl's faces on that plane, they were so excited. It was a wonderful trip, our hotel was situated right on the beach, and the weather was lovely. The girls were spoilt as there were not many children on the trip. We had busy days on the beach, and visiting other resorts such as Mihas and Fuengerola. Nights were spent dancing in the hotel, it was a holiday to remember.

Mihas is in the mountains, and the children rode on a donkey through the village, and the scenery was beautiful. I made then long dresses to wear in the evenings for the dancing. Our hotel room was a suite with a balcony, it was all so grand!

CHURCH

We went to the local Church of England Holy Trinity Church for the christening of our babies, and when Karen was around four years of age we thought she could attend Sunday School.

There were excellent leaders and I would take Karen to Sunday school, and then go into Church for the morning service. In time I understood the service and made lots of friends within the Church. As Kelly got older she joined Karen in Sunday School and I decided I would like to be confirmed. We had a Vicar in those days called Canon Radford, he had been at Kingswood for many years. I went to confirmation classes one evening per week and was sure I was doing the right thing in confirming my faith. I made myself a white dress and one summer's Sunday the Bishop came to our Church to confirm many of us from Kingswood, and the surrounding Churches. All the family attended and I felt I had their support.

I gradually became involved in numerous aspects of the Church life. Mike would take us in the car, but didn't get involved himself. However, if the children were part of anything special he would always be in the audience.

Karen became a Brownie, and gained many badges. Kelly later joined her, and then Karen moved up to the Guides. Both girls were achieving awards in all of their hobbies which retained their interest for many years.

Each Whit Monday there would be a great occasion in Kingswood of the procession of Witness. I would march with the Church and the girls would originally be sat on the lorry with the Sunday School, and later march with the Brownies and Guides. Often in the afternoon our church would hold a Fete and I would run the cake stall.

We were very proud that both Karen and Kelly gained their Queen's Guide Award, the top achievement, and it involved a lot of effort. Karen was taught by Mike's blind Uncle Arthur to read and write in Braille for one badge, which not many Guides had entered for. By this time they had transferred to Potters Wood Methodist Guide company. At Kingswood they were not inspired at Sunday School as they became older, so to keep their interest myself and a friend started a Pathfinder group for teenagers in the Church. We had a large group. Pam was a teacher so she mainly took the lessons, and I would arrange the singing and some bible study. Karen was becoming proficient playing her guitar, so would often be required to accompany the singing. Once a month in Church we had a family service, and sang more choruses, Karen joined a group of musicians to accompany the singing in Church.

The Church wardens became great friends, just like special aunties or uncles to the children. Jim, one of the wardens was extremely fond of both the girls, he was invited to their Queen's Guide Award ceremony, and eighteenth birthday parties etc. Joan, was the other warden who Kelly always presented her flowers to each Mothering Sunday, as she had never had children of her own. When Kelly left home at sixteen Joan came up to me in Church on Mothering Sunday and gave me a bunch of daffodils. I had been feeling very low and sad, and that gesture touched me greatly. It also demonstrated the love within the Church, and we knew how one another felt without speaking words. A small deed said it all.

At that time my very special friends at Church, Eileen, died from cancer. Our children had been together through Sunday School and confirmation classes. It was a very sad time, Eileen had been a very quiet, shy and inoffensive person who was a lovely Mother to her two children. What a void she left in my life, the procession would never be the same for me again, I missed her so much and still do today. She wasn't the only person I lost who was a great friend. A few years later I met Pam, she attended Church after her husband died, and the warden sat her next to me. She had two teenage daughters, and we had a lot in common. She later married again, and was very happy, and then tragedy struck in the form of mouth cancer. The first time she survived the illness, but it returned and she died.

I cleaned the brass in the Church and continued with Pathfinders for a couple of years, but once a month at the family service there was no communion, which I missed. I felt as if I was giving my all in one way or another, but spiritually I needed to receive, and eventually I stopped taking Pathfinders and became part of the congregation again.

I had started to produce wedding cakes, and was friends with an elderly master baker who I used to take to Church. He would make lovely cakes, and I would ice them. We had quite a lot of orders, as his fruit cakes and Madeira cakes were well known.

Later on he would make the girls wedding cakes for me, his cakes were very moist and he had secrets to make them so.

Linda with Karen and Kelly

KELLY, ZIGGY & LIZZY

The teenage years brought many worries with Kelly especially. She had always been strong willed, and started to oppose any authority. She was close to Mike, and tended not to annoy him on purpose. It was a different story with myself. We were both strong minded and I wouldn't give in to her demands, we continually clashed, and I was very worried about her.

Kelly was a great animal lover, and longed for a dog. At fifteen she did her work experience at Bristol Dogs Home, and saw a dog there called Ziggy. It was a cross Labrador/Bull terrier, she pleaded with her Father, who could never say no to her if she begged him, to have the dog. He said if we had the dog it would have to sleep in the shed with the rabbits, she said that would be alright, if he stayed at the Dogs home he would be put down, as no-one wanted him.

Without her knowledge, Karen & I collected him from the Home, and when Kelly arrived home from school he was waiting for her. She was overjoyed, he was a one person dog, and adored Kelly. Unfortunately he bit three times in three months, and we couldn't keep him as he was unpredictable and we could no longer take a chance, he would have to be put to sleep. He had only stayed in the shed at night for a short time, he lived in the house and we got used to owning a dog. Kelly came with us to the Dogs Home and was devastated. She brought him back and helped Mike bury him in the garden.

We had buried the rabbits in the garden as they passed away, but although she loved Bobtail nothing surpassed the grief she showed with Ziggy's death. Mike and myself knew this was the correct action but Kelly didn't see it this way. Two days after Ziggy died Kelly decided she couldn't live without a dog, she wasn't sleeping or eating and cried constantly. She saw in the local paper a dog required a good home, it was a year old, a cross beagle/smooth hair fox terrier called Lizzy. The family brought her to our home and we kept her. Kelly left home a year afterwards, but she stayed with Mike and myself, and was a wonderful companion until her old age. We loved her dearly and would take her on long country walks, and holidays were special because of her being with us.

Lizzy died February 1999, when her back legs went, and kidney disease was diagnosed. We made the agonising decision again to have a dog put to sleep. The vet came to the house as we were too upset even to drive to the surgery. This prompted me to write a poem.

We have kept her ashes in a casket, and although some people would find that morbid, to us it has had the opposite effect. We touch the casket and know a little bit of Lizzy is still with us, and gain comfort from the experience.

LIZZY

Our eyes are sore, our hearts are breaking,
We cry to ease the hurt, the aching,
We know she's gone to a peaceful place
Where she's young again to run and race.
Lizzy loved her walks in the open spaces
She knew our feelings by a glance at our faces
Happy or sad, she would cheer us no end
A loyal companion, much more than a friend.
The decision today to put her to sleep
Was hard to make, feelings run deep,
Holidays were happier because of her there,
We didn't mind the odd doggy hair.
She had the best, if only she could stay
And be with us still, now and every day
Forever incarnate, her soul will keep
We love you Lizzy, you're tired – just sleep.

KAREN & MUSIC

Neither Mike nor I are talented in the art of music. The nearest I came to playing any instrument was the tambourine in the Salvation Army. So when Karen seemed to take an interest in playing instruments it was a great joy to us, and pleasure. First in Junior school she played the recorder, then the flute. At Senior school she became interested in classical guitar and we bought her first guitar with the guidance of her guitar teacher. He was an inspiration to Karen and made playing a fun experience. It didn't always come easy to her and she worked very hard to perfect the tunes. Practising was usually an hour when she came home from school every single day. We would never have to tell her to practise, it was what she wanted to do. She told her guitar teacher that one day she wanted his job, and did not divert from that ambition, she achieved her goal. Karen is now a teacher of music. She took Grade 8 in the flute and classical guitar, and also learned to play piano and took exams for that also. This would benefit her in the future to accompany her students. We bought a keyboard for practice at home, and both girls went to piano lessons. Kelly became quite accomplished at the piano and she could have taken it further, but she played just for pleasure. Karen took it more seriously and after passing her A levels at sixth form moved on to a Music College in York for a degree in music.

It was a delight to hear Karen play the flute and guitar, her rendition of "Autumn Leaves" on the guitar was amazing. We often entertained friends, and if the girls were home we would ask then to play the keyboard or an instrument for our guests.

Whilst they were at Guides they would learn some camp songs, we would sing along and do the actions to the amusement of everyone else. We took part in an audition for the "Generation Game", the Producer came to the Guides, and I had been teaching them a routine with the tambourines. It was fun, we weren't chosen for the show, a team of majorettes were chosen instead. I am sure we would have been more entertaining after watching the others on the show.

Christmas time was usually very hectic as Karen would be playing in concerts at school, church and guides. Her Birthday on Boxing Day integrated with the festivities of Christmas. Occasionally we booked a box at the Theatre to see the Pantomime.

When Karen obtained her degree, her guitar teacher from her old school asked if she would like to take up a position as a Music teacher working abroad in St. Lucia in the Caribbean. She jumped at the chance, working at a school on this beautiful island. We took her to the airport, and she left before her degree ceremony. This was one occasion we were sorry to miss out on. Whilst there she met Andrew, who is English, and was working there as a quantity surveyor. They became a couple, and moved after two years to Barbados before coming home to settle in England.

KELLY'S ARTISTIC TALENT

I had always been interested in drawing, I drew a girl's face mostly, it wasn't good but I enjoyed the exercise. Kelly could draw well from an early age, and her work was minute detail. She would often use black pen or fine pencil for her drawings. Sometimes she copied from art books, but she could draw freehand.

We thought she could develop her skill so she attended night school for a couple of years at the Community Centre art class. Mainly adults were in the class, but there were a few children too.

She filled her portfolio and we encouraged her talent, buying all the equipment she required.

She also became interested in glass engraving, and one year etched initials on glasses to sell. She would also engrave glasses to order.

She took typing exams and passed them with flying colours so she decided she would leave school at the first opportunity and work in an office.

There she was able to show her typing ability, and in the years to follow worked as a Secretary and Personal Assistant for a well known company. Kelly has great organising ability, so she enjoyed this type of work.

MY CAKES

I baked and iced a special cake for the girl's birthdays each year. Karen's often would be a musical theme, and Kelly's artistic. I also enjoyed experimenting with Christmas cakes, so I went to a class to learn how to do it properly. I then attended another class for sugarcraft flowers, and also did a couple of day classes on a specialist subject, such as hedgerows.

This became invaluable when I progressed to making the Wedding cakes. When Mike was fifty, I arranged a surprise party for him, and I made him a cake in the shape of a typewriter. I find it quite relaxing making the sugarcraft flowers, rolling out the fine flower paste and cutting the petals as fine as I can, creating a flower which will look real. It takes hours to make enough flowers and leaves to wire up in a spray.

Not a lot of profit is made because of the time involved, and the colours have to be as near to perhaps the bridesmaids dresses as possible.

REDUNDANCY

Mike had worked for the office machine company where we met for over twenty years. He left to better himself as an office machine mechanic working for W.D. & H.O. Wills in Bristol. His friend Trevor was also employed there, and the two of them were responsible for the entire offices. Mike thought this job would be for the rest of his working life, when Hanson took over Trevor & Mike were made redundant. Mike got a job straight away for another office machine company in Bristol, but after two years Mike required an operation. Whilst recuperating we received a visit from two of the directors. They explained the company was having difficulties financially, and were having to make quite a few of the staff redundant. Mike was the last to arrive so the first to go. They took the firm's car that afternoon and paid Mike five weeks wages., no redundancy payment as he hadn't worked there long enough. I can't explain the shock we experienced. Mike wasn't well and very worried. He was out of work for eighteen months, trying endlessly for one job after another. Whilst working at Will's he had a car accident. A lorry ran into our car, and Mike was stationery at the time. He suffered a head injury and this later caused tinnitus. After a time he became deaf, we are sure it was because of the accident.

During this time of unemployment the tinnitus became worse, probably due to stress. I would go to work and return to find him in poor spirits. He made homemade beer and drank too much to drown his sorrows. Therefore I became really stressed too. Relaxation classes were suggested, and as Mike had lost a lot of confidence he said he would go if I came too. By this time I needed relaxation as much as he did, and we both benefited by attending. The teacher was excellent, and also taught and understood deaf people.

I saw a business advertised in the local paper one day for mobile car valeting, and we phoned to find out more. We had the redundancy money from Wills we had put by. After considering all aspects we knew Mike couldn't continue as he was so we ploughed all our money into buying the business.

There were few customers, and the good will we bought was non-existent. But in time Mike built the business up and it was a thriving concern. He worked extremely hard and kept it for nine years. He was dependant on the weather as he was mobile, and the winter months were the worst. He expanded by cleaning carpets and upholstery as well, so sometimes if the weather was wet, he would be glad of the inside work. Being a perfectionist he made such a good job cleaning customers cars they would book him for carpets too.

Besides my job at the surgery, and icing my wedding cakes I kept Mike's books in order, plus the banking and telephone booking in work. I received no salary, but once a year at Christmas we would go out for a meal on the business.

INSOMNIA

I've crept downstairs to make a drink
It's three o'clock, not slept a wink
My husband is snoring, so is the dog
Perhaps the duvet's too high a tog!
I've counted sheep, breathed in deep
But still I cannot get to sleep.
On a lavender pillow I lay my head
The mattress must be hard on our bed
But he's asleep but why not me?
Why should I lay awake till half past three?
I've twisted and turned, my neck is so sore
My hair's in a mess, it's becoming a bore
To still be awake night after night
And get up feeling I've been in a fight.
This cup of tea will help I'm sure
I'll try again – be asleep by four?
Then up at seven, the dog knows the time
She's like a clock without a chime!
It's Christmas Eve tomorrow, lots to do
Hope I don't fall asleep in the pew!
Tomorrow night!

OLIVE

My Mum, Olive, lived until she was eighty-three. She married for the third time in the early seventies, but divorced later. Whilst she was married they moved from my Grandparents house to a council flat. When the marriage collapsed Mum lived between Janet and myself for six months, until she had a flat of her own. We visited frequently and she saw the grandchildren a lot, but we noticed she wasn't cooking for herself very much. She was advised by her doctor to go into sheltered accommodation, which she did for a couple of years. Whilst there she suffered small strokes (TIA's) and again stopped caring for herself. It was upsetting for Janet and myself as Mum had always been very smart and a brilliant cook. We would take food, put it in the fridge, and days later it would still be there. Mum was then admitted to a Residential home, just around the corner from where I worked at the surgery. After a few years there, she had more strokes, mainly at night, and the home didn't have the facilities or staff to cope, so she moved again to a Nursing home. After being there six months she had a massive stroke which left her in a coma for six weeks. She went into hospital but they could do no more for her, so she went back to the Home to die. I look back on her life and realise what a hard time she had, bringing us up on her own, losing two husbands at an early age, and looking after her elderly and infirm parents. She had a sense of humour and when she could let her hair down and enjoy herself she had no inhibitions. She loved to attend the Salvation Army, and she loved to sing. Her favourite hymn was "The Old Rugged Cross" which we had played at her funeral held at the Salvation Army.

Now the children had no grandparents left but each have wonderful memories of a very loving Grandmother.

One instance we will always remember was near the end of her life, at the Nursing Home. Olive always loved male company, and a new resident was admitted. She had her hair set, and they were in the garden talking. Without the consent of the Matron, and taking into consideration neither could hardly put one foot in front of the other, they absconded! They crossed over a busy main road arm in arm to the local pub. This gave the Matron and staff concern, and it took staff and patients to find them. The following day Janet took Mum out in her wheelchair to the shopping centre for a coffee. "I had a lovely time last night!" Mum said. Janet thought she had enjoyed a sing-song at the Home, until Mum explained rather sheepishly that she had absconded with the new man for a drink. Janet apologised profusely to the Matron on their return, as if taking back a naughty schoolgirl. It was taken in good heart with Matron explaining to my sister it was residents like Mum who kept the place alive! My friend tells me whenever she drives past the Home, she can see in her mind's eye the two of them hobbling across the road. Mum wasn't a Soldier in the Salvation Army, so she enjoyed a drink at times.

My mother, Olive

JANET

As we grew older Janet and I became much closer. After our marriages and having children we had much more in common. Janet and Pete had a girl Paula, and then a boy Matthew. We would get together at weekends sometimes, and always at Christmas or bank holidays take it in turn to entertain, with Mum included.

Sadly Janet's marriage broke down, and when the children left home they divorced. Janet met her second husband Ted, and they were happy for a while, until Ted was shot in the eye from boys holding an air gun rifle. He lost an eye, and their life changed. They divorced but were still in touch with one another.

Ironically, Ted was mugged yet again and fell into bushes. His good eye was infected badly and couldn't be saved, and he became blind. This tragedy brought them back together. Her children meanwhile had both married, and Janet now has her grandchildren to enjoy.

Janet, Ted and Usca

A PURPOSE IN LIFE

Whilst the girls were young I tried working weekends at Marks and Spencer, then I found an office job where they granted me school holidays free. One day a friend from Church asked me to fill in for her job as a doctor's receptionist. She was to have an operation. This I did and enjoyed it so much, working for a single handed female GP who was the same age as myself. My friend didn't return to the job and I was employed permanently part-time. This lasted for approx. twenty-six years. The surgery was the old fashioned type with no appointments. I gradually knew all the families, four generations in some instances, and the atmosphere there was so friendly.

The doctor I worked for was deaf herself, and she suggested Mike attended lip-reading classes as she had done. Mike enrolled in an evening lip-reading class, and wanted me to accompany him as he had lost his confidence since becoming deaf. I went with him for five years, and then he attended on his own. His lipreading teacher's husband had a hearing-dog for the deaf, and suggested to Mike that he applied for one.

I continued to work at the surgery until my employer merged with another surgery nearby. I worked there for a while before I retired. It didn't have the atmosphere of my previous surgery as it was big with many doctors. Giving appointments wasn't always easy, and often patients were irate because they couldn't obtain an appointment, or were waiting so long. This was unusual for me and I found it quite stressful. So when I reached retirement age I left.

FLINT

In the meantime Mike had his application accepted by Hearing dogs for Deaf People. We waited eighteen months, until he was partnered with Flint, a year old lab x greyhound. In 2000 he went to the training centre for her last week of training to bond with her and train. She is the most gentle dog I have ever known with a wonderful temperament. Flint had been handed in at eight weeks old to the RSPCA in Southampton, and trained by hearing dogs until she was nearly a year old. She changed Mike's life, and made him confident enough to give talks to raise money for the charity. This, with my help kept us busy, and also the opportunity to meet some lovely people. Flint responds to all the noises in the house which Mike cannot hear, such as the telephone, doorbell, clock alarm, cooker timer and smoke alarm. She is trained to touch him, and then take him to the source of the sound, except for the smoke alarm, when he has to investigate the danger himself. As an assistance dog she accompanies him everywhere. When we go on holiday she comes too, and Flint is admired wherever she goes.

I have had to take a back seat, and allow Flint to tell Mike the sounds. She has taken over his life, and he is absolutely besotted with her. We joined the local Branch just after having her, and after a while I became Secretary. We raised thousands of pounds for the charity with our talks, and many deaf people received a dog and because of Flint, we were able to raise so much because of her being at the talks and shows.

LEAN ON ME

Mike is deaf, and could hear no more
The telephone or a knock on the door
Until one day his life was enriched
With Flint, with whom he is bewitched
She's gentle, always by his side
To tell him sounds, his constant guide.
Flint was selected from many breeds
To match with Mike, to meet his needs.
The last two years the bond has grown
She's done much more than answer the phone

Flint is accompanying Mike on his talks
She gets rewarded with treats and long walks.
Raising money for Hearing Dogs is their aim
It takes so much to rescue and train.
Their picture on leaflets, Crufts, and in the press
Has made them famous, Flint deserves no less
For the work she's doing day by day
Carry on the good work is what we say
Keep going Mike, to spread the word
With your devoted friend, he hasn't heard
But Flint does, and lets him know
She lifts his spirit when feeling low
The photographer captured the trust, together
Her paw on Mike's shoulder, friends forever.

Mike with Flint

I wrote this poem when we had Flint for two years, and the photograph was taken in London for the leaflets. This wonderful photograph which shows the bond so clearly has been used on so much publicity. In newspaper and magazine articles, theatre programmes, postcards etc. The photograph was unveiled at Crufts in 2002, when the look and the logo changed for Hearing Dogs. It was used on the Annual report, we were very proud that from all of the hearing dogs all over the country, it was Flint they chose for the front cover. An enlarged photo was also pride of place behind the reception desk at the Headquarters, at the Grange, in Princes Risborough, Buckinghamshire. We try to attend this centre when they have an open day in the summer, and we meet old friends with hearing dogs there, and make new friends.

Everyone knows Flint as her photograph with Mike has become famous. I take a selection of publicity literature when we give talks, as people are very interested, and usually extremely generous. Besides the donation notes are often put in the collecting box, this is how we have been able to raise so much money for this wonderful charity, which not only rescues the dogs, but also the deaf recipient.

Mike collecting a cheque from the Freemasons of Bristol

VOLUNTEER OF THE YEAR AWARD

Our regional co-ordinator for Hearing Dogs, Marilyn, entered Mike for a Volunteer of the Year Award in 2005. He had been working hard giving talks and shows, and deserved the accolade.

We were invited to the Mansion House in Bristol where the Lord Lieutenant of Bristol presented the medals to numerous people who had done outstanding work for charities.

It was an unexpected honour, and I felt very proud as Mike received the medal, together with Flint of course!

Mike, Flint and Myself at a Council House Show in Bristol, in front of our stand of goods for sale.

This prompted me to write the following:-

Mike has received a Volunteer of the Year Award
Presented by the Lord Lieutenant in his uniform, and sword
Lots of winners there from many walks of life
Mike took Flint, his hearing dog, and also Lin his wife.
Before each person had their medal a little speech was said
Of how they helped their community, some faces were bright red!
But all felt proud of their achievements, acknowledged in this way

A medal from the Royal Mint has really made their day
To treasure from this moment, and keep for ever more
To show to friends and family, not keep it in a drawer.
This gives them the encouragement and maybe plant a seed
For folk to give time freely, and help others more in need.

What a difference this little dog, Flint has made to both our lives. We have met good friends, visited lovely places, and had such a feeling of well being for helping such a deserving charity. Deaf people are often isolated, and lonely, and these hearing dogs bring them out of their loneliness, and into the world once again. Dogs are certainly man's best friend.

GRANDCHILDREN

Karen married Andrew and they have two lovely girls, Rebecca, and Sarah, who have both inherited Karen's talent for music. They live in Warwick so unfortunately we don't see them very often. Karen tries to visit us with the girls in the school holidays.

Sarah and Rebecca

Kelly married David, and had two boys, Theo and Louis. Unfortunately David left when Louis was five, and Theo eight. Both boys are on the autistic spectrum, and Theo has Aspergers syndrome.

Kelly was distraught on her own, and eventually sold the house, and rented next door to us. We could be there for one another. Kelly loves animals, and got the boys a dog called Ebony. She is very gentle and has made an enormous difference.

Our four grandchildren are very special to us, and we look forward to watching their lives unfold for many years to come.

Louis

Theo

A SOLDIER AT LAST

Not long after having Flint in 2000 we met a lady from the Salvation Army whilst shopping in a supermarket. She explained that the annual Carol Concert would soon be taking place in the Colston Hall in Bristol. The Army hadn't yet decided on the charities they would choose to benefit from the goodwill collection. We applied and were accepted, which meant Mike doing a short presentation on stage with Flint twice in one day. The Carol Concert was on the Sunday afternoon, and again in the evening. We were very nervous, but Mike spoke well, and Flint made a good impression wagging her tail at the vast audience. We were presented with a cheque for £3,500 and the other charity chosen, the Neonatal Unit of a local Hospital received the same amount. This was a wonderful start to our fundraising. Members of the band invited us to their Corps any Sunday we wished to attend. Obviously I was keen as having loved the Army in my youth. We occasionally attended and Mike enjoyed the meetings, and the welcome we received. Flint loved the band, and totally relaxed when the music started. Music is so well played, not only the band, but the Songsters, Singing Company, and Junior band.

This was nine years ago, and over time has meant more and more to me. I made the big decision to become a Soldier myself. I attended recruitment class, and I was enrolled in September 2009. My faith has always been strong, and this commitment cements that. I purchased my uniform, not the bonnet as in the olden days but a type of bowler hat for the ladies.

Friends and family who know me are not surprised I took this step. We had our house on the market and would have liked to move to Dorset. Little did I realise my life would take a different path from now on, with the Salvation Army at the core. Although Mike had enjoyed his attendance at the Army meetings, when I explained I wanted to be a Soldier he resented it. Since he became deaf my life had revolved around helping him, in his business, Hearing Dog talks, lip-reading etc. This was something I wanted to do "for myself". He refused to come to the Army, and gradually made my life unbearable. He had been drinking heavily for years, but this became worse and I suffered verbal abuse every day. On the day of my enrolment as a Soldier he spoilt it completely for me, and this made me realise I needed to take a drastic step. Mike constantly told me to get a divorce, and I did. I moved out of the home I had lived in for nearly 45 years in October 2009, and I live alone in a rented flat where I am very happy. Being a Soldier I now help the Salvation Army in a voluntary way, helping to cook lunches for the over 60's, and doing whatever I can. The Army have been a wonderful support to me in this stage of my life., and I know God will take care of me.

Me in my new uniform

A NEW LIFE

Becoming a Soldier made me strong in more ways than I could ever imagine. When I had made the decision to take this step I told Mike, making it clear I could continue giving talks for Hearing Dogs, plus volunteering for the Army, as I now had retired. He took the news very badly and resented my involvement straight away. He refused to come to the Army, as we used to, and made it difficult for me to attend, even to my recruitment lessons. But the more I learned, the more I wanted this in my life.

Karen and Rebecca   **Theo reads my poem**

Since he became deaf our life had revolved around his needs, I had attended relaxation and lip reading classes with him and I was happy to give talks. This decision of becoming a Soldier meant I was fulfilling a need in me and he became angry and drank more. On the day I was enrolled as a Soldier he spoilt it completely, reducing me to tears on the journey to the ceremony. I had waited for this day since the age of sixteen, and I was devastated I didn't have his support. Karen played the classical guitar and Rebecca the flute to Massenet's "Meditation" during the ceremony, and Theo read my poem "Comfort".

I gave my testimony and read "A Soldier at last". I should have felt so happy but inwardly I felt so upset that I didn't have Mike's blessing.

A SOLDIER AT LAST

What can I give to the One who died for me?
What can I offer in exchange for Calvary?
My experiences of life I can hopefully share
With others whose burdens are heavy to bear.
An outstretched hand or a kindly touch
If offered in friendship means so much.
I'm sure my remaining years I could share
My trust in the Lord, make others aware
That God loves them too, in Him they will find
A much happier life and a peaceful mind.
I reflect my childhood many years before
As a Junior Soldier in the Fishponds Corps.
And now in the Autumn of my life
I've been a mother, I've been a wife.
Now Jesus has wrapped His arms around me,
A Soldier at last! My spirit is free.
He's Winter and Summer, Autumn and Spring,
In fact God is real, He's in everything!

At the family gathering afterwards I realised that Mike did not love me at all, he completely spoilt this very special day in my life.

When he had too much to drink during our marriage, and I admonished him he would tell me to get a divorce. I had tried to get him help but he would never admit there was a problem. For the last few years I had found hidden bottles in the garage and shed. When a persons' life revolves around drink the whole family is affected, and this destroys love and respect. If Mike had admitted there was a problem and tried to address the fact alcohol ruled his life, I would have stayed. Now I needed to make a happier life for myself, and hoped I had the strength to move out. In less than two months I had found a flat, and left, as my life was becoming unbearable. I purchased second-hand furniture, and whilst making all these arrangements Mike took my name off the car insurance so I couldn't use the car any longer. Kelly was a wonderful support at this time, and helped me in numerous ways. My flat is spacious and in a good position for bus routes, and shops. I began divorce proceedings, and after I left I missed Flint greatly, but knew for peace of mind I had done the best action possible.

Visit to Canada

I have a second cousin, and his wife who live in Ontario, Canada. They were concerned to hear of my situation and offered me a holiday, the flight being paid for by their air miles, to stay with them in Canada,

This gave me something to look forward to, and I had a wonderful time. I loved Canada and they took me to various sight-seeing delights including Niagara Falls, the CN Tower in Toronto, and Stratford. Their home is New Hamburg in a retirement complex with fantastic amenities, where we used the swimming pool nearly every day. For three weeks I enjoyed their company, and I was so grateful for this opportunity.

I like to look smart but I have never been slim, but slightly overweight. For years Mike daily called me "grotesque" which was soul destroying.

Once on my own I joined weight watchers and lost the two stone I needed to. At goal weight I felt great, and I did this for myself, not him.

WEIGHT WATCHERS

I'm watching my weight like a hawk
I'm boring myself when I talk!
I'm cutting out this & cutting out that
And adapting my meals to be LOW FAT
Yet it's certainly good for the soul
Now a few pounds away from my goal.

I've tracked and weighed, I live in hope
I've even bought a skipping rope
I line dance and swim
To keep myself trim…
Oh! My dress size now has reduced
And my jeans feel amazingly loose.

By Christmas I hope to look slimmer
I will relish my Christmas dinner
But next year I aim
That my weight stays the same.
Folks say I look younger
I've no pangs of hunger
Overweight is a NO NO again.

At the Army I began to help cooking lunches for the over 60's some Thursdays. I also helped on Christmas days providing lunch and hospitality to people who would otherwise been alone. Being a Soldier encourage me to help collecting when the band play carols in the City.

So proud to wear my uniform and belong to the Army, to witness my faith to others and show how God is part of my life. My trust in Him has made me complete. Many friends at the Army gave me lifts to the Corps on Sundays and Thursdays, but after two years I eventually received a small settlement from the Solicitor, and I have purchased a second-hand car. I continue to make special occasion cakes to enable me to run the car, plus I enjoy the hobby, especially creating the sugar flowers.

DOGS

Both daughters, Karen and Kelly have been supportive and although I don't see Karen so often, as they live away, Kelly and the boys I see regularly. Kelly has always loved animals, and has purchased a dog from a rescue centre, and named her Ebony. This dog has brought devotion from the boys and helped Theo in particular with his Autism; and Asperger's Syndrome.

EBONY

We wished for a dog, we waited a while
And when we saw her she made us smile
A little black puppy, one half of her a lab
Mixed with German shepherd, we thought she was fab.
"Ebony" suited her when we gave her a name
She responded well, we called, she came.
As a rescue dog, she now feels secure
When we enter the house she bounds through the door
She's ever so quiet, hardly a bark
Her coat has brown stripes now amongst the dark.
We took her to classes for her to be trained
Ebony learned quickly, her confidence gained
When we return from school she is always there
We've learnt to groom her, and how to care
For our "booful" companion whom we all love
We should offer a prayer to our Father above
She's gentle in nature, so relaxed in a crowd
And in the dog show she made us proud!
Ebony won three rosettes and got best in show
She came home a queen, "she knows you know"
Walking round the ring she kept by our side
She realises she's special, we're full of pride.
In the garden when tired of games we played
She finds a bush and sleeps in the shade
Then wakes and wildly chases the butterflies
But gentleness gleams in her lovely eyes
She's brought such joy, and much less stress
In each of our lives she has truly blessed

Ebony lifts her paw, a wet kiss she'll share
You sent her, God, and we thank you in prayer

After four years Kelly then rescued another little dog "Buddy" for Louis. Although I no longer have a dog I enjoy seeing Ebony and Buddy.

BUDDY

Buddy is Ebony's shadow
You follow her everywhere
You were rescued by the charity
When no-one seemed to care
Buddy lived in a cage, you were never trained
To walk with a lead, or to play
So now Louis loves you and gently shows
He cares for you day by day.
Ebony is teaching the rules of the home
Where to drink, eat, play and rest
And after these lessons are learnt
Be a model dog – one of the best!
And belong to a family who don't have wealth
But love in abundance and joy
To look after you always, and show you how
To behave well, you beautiful boy.

Around the time I moved into my flat, my sister and her husband moved away from Bristol. Ted being blind has a guide dog, Usca, and I see them quite often. Dogs add a special quality to a family by their loyalty.

Ebony and Buddy with Louis and Theo

PEACE

After a forty-five year marriage I have witnessed that by the grace of God we can overcome life's challenges. I rarely feel alone, I know that I am in my Fathers' care and I trust that I continue to prove to myself "I am strong in the strength of the Lord" as the old song says. It has taken me two years to wear my wedding and engagement rings on my other hand. After such a long marriage I cannot remove them entirely.

I purchased an ornament, white letters spelling PEACE and wrote this poem explaining what it means to me, I have peace in my heart and my life.

PEACE

Walking along the High Street I noticed a shop
Displaying trinkets & gifts which caused me to stop
Beautiful words each spelling a letter
Wherever I looked I could not have found better.
I entered the shop and enquired the price
The answer, reasonable, the surprise was nice.
Of all the words, PEACE, I chose and bought
The significance, deep meaning, my attention was caught.
This sign sits on my wall unit for all to see
It is greatly admired, but most of all by me
The white letters are clear, they stand proud and tall
Which is how I should feel, not topple or fall?
They convey to me I now have peace of mind
Which above all I cherish, inner peace I find.
A surprising fact that a single word can impress
Change and alter our mind, and reduce our stress.

Linda Sullivan
July 2011.